FROM PICTURES TO WORDS

A Book About Making a Book

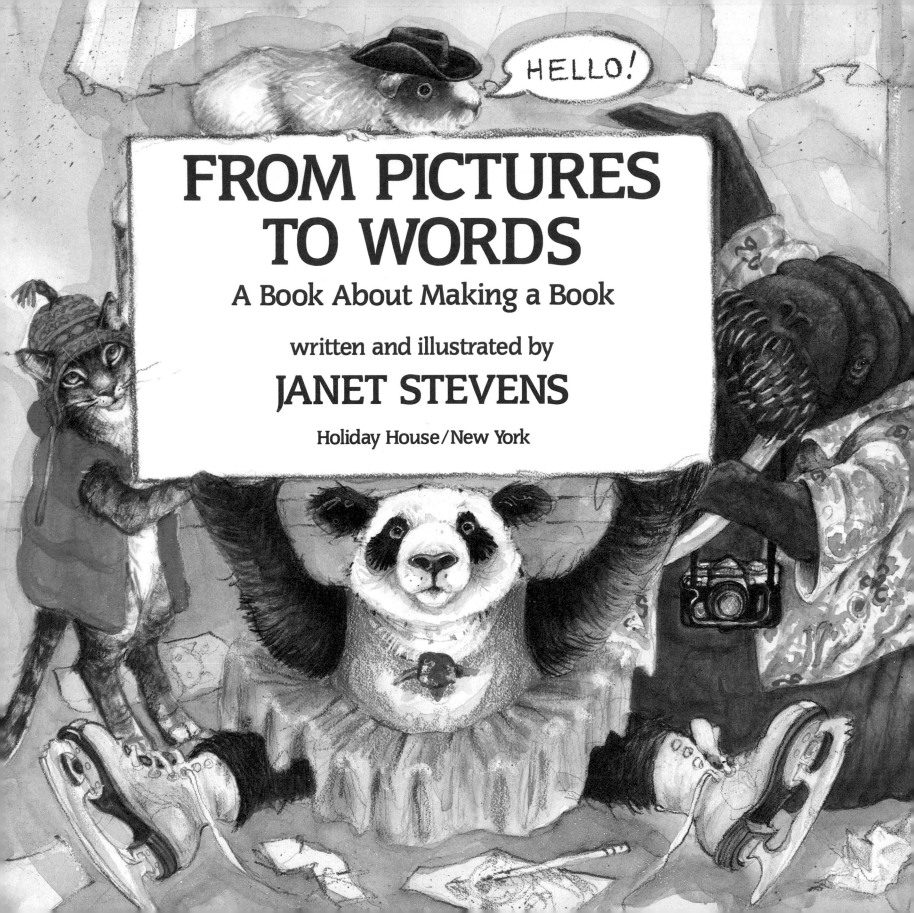

To the young authors and illustrators around the country—
and for Susie and my dad.

Library of Congress Cataloging-in-Publication Data
Stevens, Janet.
From pictures to words : a book about making a book / Janet Stevens.
p.   cm.
ISBN 0-8234-1154-0
1. Stevens, Janet—Themes, motives—Juvenile literature.
2. Picture books for children—United States—Juvenile literature.
[1. Authorship.   2. Creative writing.   3. Stevens, Janet.
4. Authors, American.   5. Illustrators.]   I. Title.
NC975.5.S74A4   1994   94-18976
CIP   AC   741.6'42'092—dc20
ISBN 0-8234-1271-7 (pbk.)

PSST... REMEMBER US?

"Hello, my name is Janet Stevens, and I am an illustrator. Drawing pictures for books is my job. Authors write the words, then I do the artwork."

"Psst. Psst. J-a-a-a-n-e-t."

"What? Who's there?"

"We're the characters in your imagination talking. We think it's about time *you* wrote a story for *us*."

"I draw pictures. I can't write stories!"

"You can if you try! Come on, we're all dressed up with no place to go. We need to be in a book. We want something exciting to do. We need places to go, people to meet. We're like actors without a stage, burgers without buns, aliens without spaceships!"

"But writing is hard for me. I don't know if I can write a story."
"We'll help. Come on, please?"
"OK, OK, but don't expect too much."
"Super! Can we all be in the story?"
"I don't think so. My story would get too crowded with all of you. How about I just use three of you—Koala Bear, Cat, and Rhino. You've been in my imagination the longest."
"YES!"
"Now what?" I ask.

"No, I'd rather set the story in the mountains near where I live," I say.

"What will we do? What is the *plot*? We need action, mystery, an adventure," says Koala.

"I have another idea. I think you should all go on a camping trip," I say.

"A camping trip? Yuck! That's boring!" says Koala.

"I like camping! Last summer, I went with friends and it was so funny! We couldn't agree where to set up camp. After wandering around the mountains for hours, we finally found the perfect spot—our own backyard! Maybe I could use that idea in my story," I suggest.

"That might work," says Rhino.

"Let me try. I'll make some sketches right now to help me think. I need to figure out the story's beginning, middle, and end."

BEGINNING

MIDDLE

CAMPSITE #1

CAMPSITE #2

"CUT! This story's boring!" says Koala. "Most of it is a lot of yak, yak, yak about finding the perfect camping spot. Nothing really happens, except that we end up camping in our own backyard. You need to add a *problem*, tension, and drama!"

"How about adding a blizzard or an avalanche?" says Rhino.
"Or maybe an alien spaceship lands and kidnaps us!" says Cat.

"I like the idea of a blizzard best. That's a good problem. How about: you get stranded on the mountain in a blizzard."

"Then what? How do we solve the problem? How do we get home?" asks Rhino.

"I know, you could use your special talents and skills and work together," I say.

"Koala is smart and she could think up a good plan. Rhino is big and you could all ride on his back. Cat is small and a good climber. She could scramble up trees and see what lies ahead. You could help each other get home safely."

ONE PIZZA WITH PEPPERONI.

"What happens next? Hey, I know. When we all get home, we are tired and hungry. We decide to order pizza. But, just like we couldn't decide on the perfect spot, we can't decide which topping to order," says Koala.

BLA-A-K, I HATE PEPPERONI. I WANT BLACK OLIVE.

GROSS, NOT BLACK OLIVE.

"But I get my choice because I'm the biggest and strongest," says Rhino.

"Rhino! Didn't you learn anything from our adventure? We must cooperate!" says Koala.

"Right—we must order something that everyone likes—maybe the deluxe super-duper supreme big-pleaser special," says Rhino.

"YES! The aliens can deliver it!" yells Cat.

"NO," I yell.

NO!

PIZZA

"I think this story might work. I'll try laying it out in a storyboard."
"What's that?"
"It's a map of the book—like a comic strip—that shows all thirty-two pages on a single piece of paper."

1 (½ TITLE PAGE)   2 (FULL TITLE PAGE)   3   4 (COPYRIGHT-DEDICATION PAGE)   (STORY BEGINS) 5

6   7   8   9   10   11

12   13   14   15   16   17

"When I'm making my storyboard, sometimes I pretend I'm a video camera," I say.

"I can zoom in real close . . .

or closer . . .

or zoom out."

"I've finally finished the storyboard," I say. "Now that I have a story in pictures, I can start writing the words. It will take me a while to get the text just the way I want it. I'll have to write and rewrite."

"Go for it," says Koala.

The Perfect Spot
by
Janet Stevens

Cat was bored. "I hate these Saturdays," she said, "when I just can't figure out what to do."

"I think it's a camping kind of day," said Koala. "Let's head for the mountains!"

"Look outside," said Rhino. "It's cloudy. It's terrible to camp when there's no sun."

"The paper says the weather's going to clear up and be picture perfect," said Koala.

"Oh, what does the paper know?" said Cat. "When it's cloudy, there isn't any sun, and when there is no sun, it's cold. I'm freezing just thinking about it."

"Now, come on, camping is a great idea. Let's get moving, and I'm sure you'll warm up," said Koala.

The three campers pulled out all of the equipment and arranged it on the floor. There were tents, sleeping bags, air mattresses, stoves, lawn chairs, umbrellas, and backpacks.

HEY, I LIKE THE TITLE.

GREAT, BUT NO ALIENS.

DID SHE SPELL KOALA RIGHT?

A few days go by . . .

"Phew. I'm done. It took me a long time, but it was easier than I thought."

"I'll run down to the post office and send it to my editor in New York. If she and the other people at the publishing house like it, it will get published."

"How long will it take for them to decide?" asks Koala.

"You never know."

Weeks go by . . .

Then the phone rings.

"It's my editor! She likes my story! She says they want to publish it, but it needs a few changes."

"We like it the way it is," says Koala.
"Don't worry. She's made some good suggestions. As soon as she mails the manuscript back, I'll get to work again," I explain.
And I do. It takes me several days to make changes.

"I hope my editor will be happy with the revisions I've done. I just faxed her the changes I made."

I talk to my editor for a few minutes.
"She likes my changes!" I yell. "She says I can start the dummy as soon as she sends me the type."

"This spot is too windy. Look, everything is blowing away!" cries Koala.
"At least it's cool," says Rhino.
"Let's move on," says Cat.

"A dummy is a practice book," I explain. "It's a book I make with sketch paper that is the same size as the final book. I cut apart the type once I get it in the mail. I tape it down on the pages of the dummy so I'll know how much space it will take up. Using my storyboard map, I take the little sketches I made earlier and draw them larger on the sketch paper. When I'm done, I have a rough idea of what the final book will look like."

It takes me about a week to make the dummy.

"Do you have to send it to that editor lady again?" asks Rhino.

"Yes, I'm on my way to the post office now."

A few more weeks go by. Then my editor sends my dummy back, with more suggestions.

"What's next?" asks Koala.

"Finally, I can get out my good paper and start the finished artwork."

"Show us how you do it."

"I have to decide whether I want to use watercolor, colored pencils, or maybe colored pencils on brown paper.

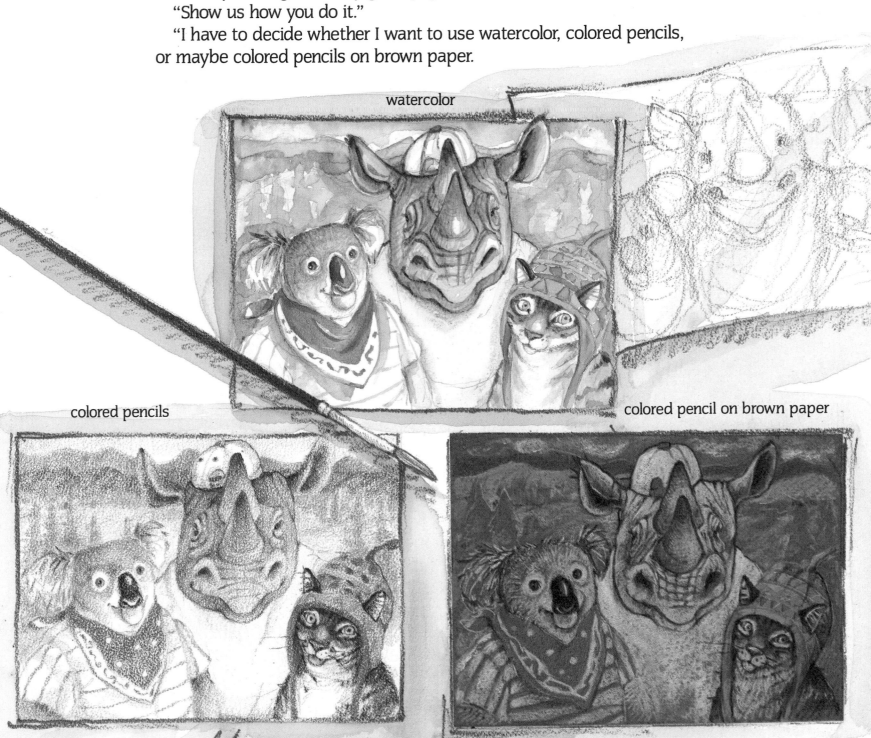

watercolor

colored pencils

colored pencil on brown paper

"I could draw you loose with markers . . . or make you flat, like a cartoon.

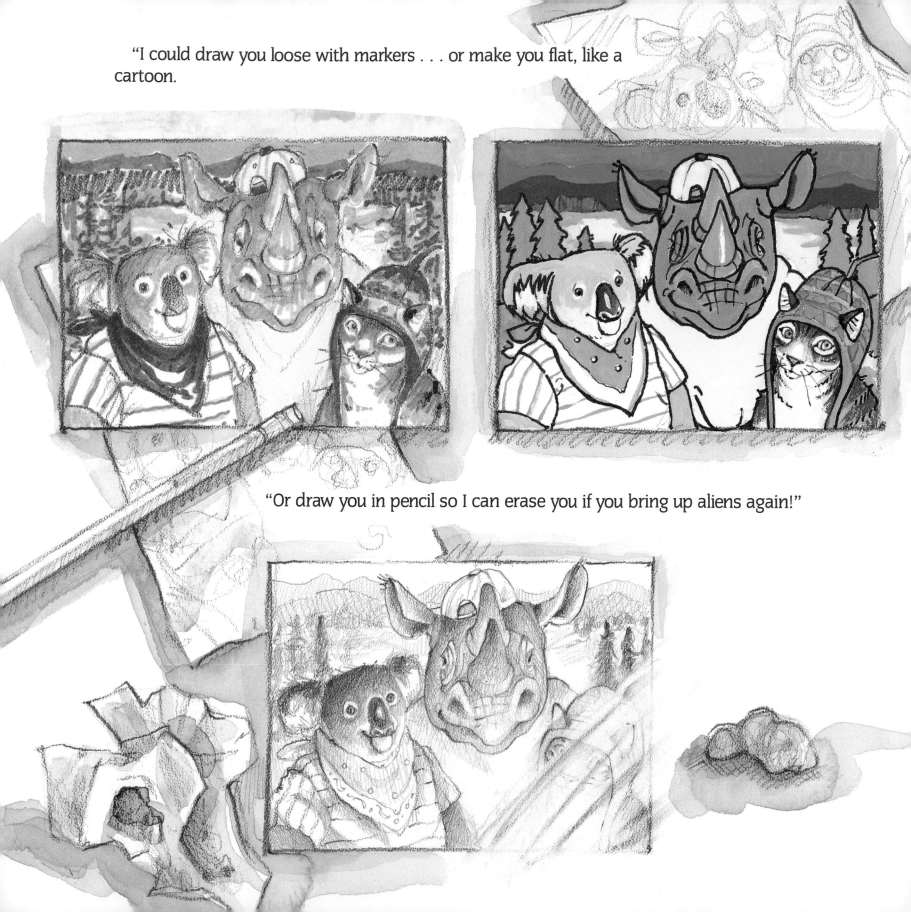

"Or draw you in pencil so I can erase you if you bring up aliens again!"

"I think I'll paint the book in watercolor and add some colored pencil.

I like the way this looks. I'll keep working on it."

"How long will it take you to do the artwork?"
"A long time," I say.
"And then what will happen?"
"I'll send it to New York again. It will get printed on a big printing press and eventually, we'll all see a finished book."

"We did it," I say. "Our book is being published. I couldn't have done it without you."

"There are other ways to develop a story. You might start with the plot instead of the character. Or you might start with the ending, then work your way back to the beginning. In this book, I simply shared one way to do it.

"Maybe you'd like to take one of my other characters and write a story. Or maybe you can create your own.

"Here's a list of a few things you need to remember:

title—what the story is called

character—person in the story

plot—what happens

setting—where the story takes place

problem—the situation in the story that needs solving

"Have fun!"